RICHARD ARMITAGE
for Farworlds Ltd.
presents

ME AND MY GIRL

The Leicester Haymarket production

ROBERT LINDSAY

FRANK THORNTON

RICHARD CALDICOT **SUSANNAH FELLOWS** **ROBERT LONGDEN**
ROY MACREADY **MYRA SANDS** and **URSULA SMITH**
with
EMMA THOMPSON as 'Sally'

Book and lyrics by
L. ARTHUR ROSE & DOUGLAS FURBER

Music by
NOEL GAY

Book revised by STEPHEN FRY   Contribution to revisions by MIKE OCKRENT

Set design by
MARTIN JOHNS

Costume designs by
ANN CURTIS

Lighting design by
CHRIS ELLIS

Production
Musical Director
CHRIS WALKER

Musical
Director
IAN HUGHES

Sound
design by
RICK CLARK

Choreography by
GILLIAN GREGORY

Directed by
MIKE OCKRENT

First Published 1984
© International Music Publications

Exclusive Distributors
International Music Publications

ME AND MY GIRL

ME AND MY GIRL

ME AND MY GIRL

Words by DOUBLAS FURBER
Music by NOEL GAY

Refrain

Me and my girl,___ Meant for each o - ther, sent for each o - ther, and

C   Em   C   G+ Am   C   G+ Am   C#°

lik - ing it so___ Me and my girl,___ 'Sno use pre - tend - ing, we knew the end

G7   Dm7 G7 Dm7   G7   Dm7 Fm G7

- ing some a - ges a - go.___ Some lit - tle church with a big stee - ple,

G+   C   C   Em   C   G+ Am

Just a few peo - ple that both of us know___ And we'll have love, laughter, be

C   E7   A7   C#°   Dm   F   Fm   Ab°

1.   2.

hap-py ev - er af - ter, Me and my girl.___ girl.___

C   E7   A7   D7   Dm7 G   C   Dm7 G7   C

LAMBETH WALK

Words by DOUGLAS FURBER
Music by NOEL GAY

LEANING ON A LAMP-POST

Words and Music
by NOEL GAY

LOVE MAKES THE WORLD GO ROUND

Words and Music
by NOEL GAY

ONCE YOU LOSE YOUR HEART

Words and Music
by NOEL GAY

THINKING OF NO ONE BUT ME

Words by DOUGLAS FURBER
Music by NOEL GAY

THE SUN HAS GOT HIS HAT ON
(He's Coming Out Today)

Words and Music by
RALPH BUTLER and NOEL GAY

Printed by Halstan & Co. Ltd., Amersham, Bucks., England